About this book

Air is vital to life. People, animals and plants breathe it. Air has weight, it is able to exert pressure, and it can be squeezed into small containers. Moving air causes the winds. Birds fly on air and so do machines. You can find out how amazing air is by doing the experiments in this book. If you are not familiar with something you need for an experiment, look on pp.6-7 for an explanation. Always read 'Laboratory procedure' on p.7 before you start an experiment.

Contents

Cover illustration Tom Stimpson

Series editor Wendy Boase
Designer Alan Baron

Copyright © 1982 by Walker Books Ltd

First published in Great Britain in 1982 by
Methuen Children's Books Ltd, in association
with Walker Books.

Printed in the United States of America
First U.S. Edition
1 2 3 4 5 6 7 8 9 10
2 3 4 5 6 7 8 9 10 11 (pbk)

Library of Congress Catalog Card
Number 82-80991

ISBN 0-688-00977-8 (pap.)
ISBN 0-688-00973-5 (lib. bdg.)

Amazing Air

Written by
Henry Smith

Step-by-step illustrations by
Barbara Firth and Rosalinda Kightley

Feature illustrations by
Elizabeth Falconer

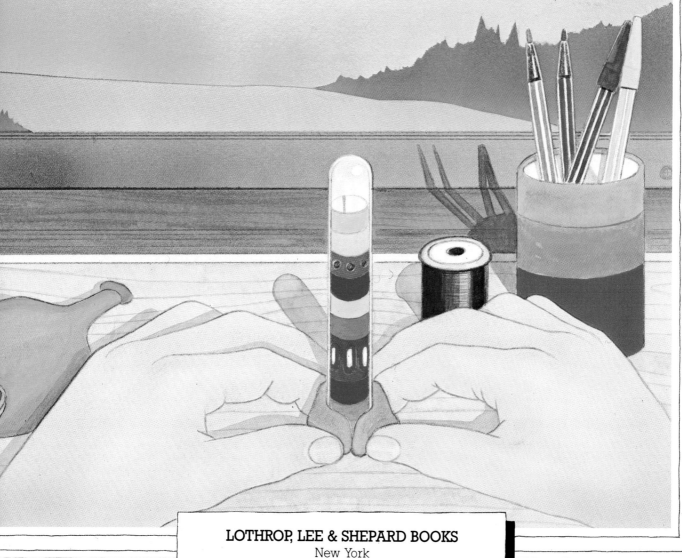

LOTHROP, LEE & SHEPARD BOOKS
New York

Supplies and skills

Basic materials

You don't need a lot of special equipment to experiment at home. Clear a special shelf or cupboard and start collecting some basic, inexpensive materials for your home laboratory.

Sheets of white and coloured paper and card.

Clean, glass jam and pickle jars.

Empty washing-up liquid bottles.

Sheets of newspaper, brown paper or old wrapping paper.

Penknife, ruler and scissors.

Soft (B or 2B) and hard (3H) pencils.

Pair of compasses.

Cotton thread, paper clips and drawing pins.

Other materials

If you are not familiar with a particular material or piece of equipment you need for an experiment, look for it in the following list.

Balsa wood is very lightweight. This, and **balsa wood glue**, can be bought at an art or craft shop.

Bamboo or cane sticks are very thin and lightweight. Buy them at a garden centre or florist's shop.

Batteries are sold at electrical or radio shops. A battery's electrical energy is measured in volts. Electricity is taken from a battery via its terminals.

Bungs are like rubber corks. Some are made with holes in them. Buy bungs at a chemist's or in shops that sell wine-making equipment.

Cling film is a thin, transparent wrapping that sticks to surfaces. Buy it at a supermarket.

Clips, bulldog are used to hold papers. Buy them at a stationery shop. **Crocodile clips** are used on electrical circuits. Buy these at a hardware or electrical shop.

A curtain ring can be bought from a haberdasher's or department store.

Dowelling is like a round wooden stick. Buy it at a hardware shop.

Enamel paint is used to paint metal surfaces. You can buy it at craft shops and some hardware shops.

Evaporated milk is thick and creamy. Buy it from a supermarket or grocery shop.

Fabric glue can be bought at a haberdasher's or a craft shop.

Filter funnels can be bought from a chemist, the science section of a large toy shop, or a shop that sells wine-making equipment.

Flex, 1-core plastic-covered is the kind that has strands of fine wire inside a plastic covering. Buy it at electrical or radio shops.

Food dyes colour food. Buy them at a supermarket or grocery shop.

Glasspaper is a special paper which has finely ground minerals stuck to it. It is used to smooth wood. Buy it at a hardware shop.

Insulating tape is sold at electrical or hardware shops. It is thick and strong.

Masking tape won't leave a mark if peeled off gently. Buy it at an art or craft shop.

A metal punch can be bought at a hardware shop.

A modelling knife has a very sharp blade. Buy it at an art or craft shop.

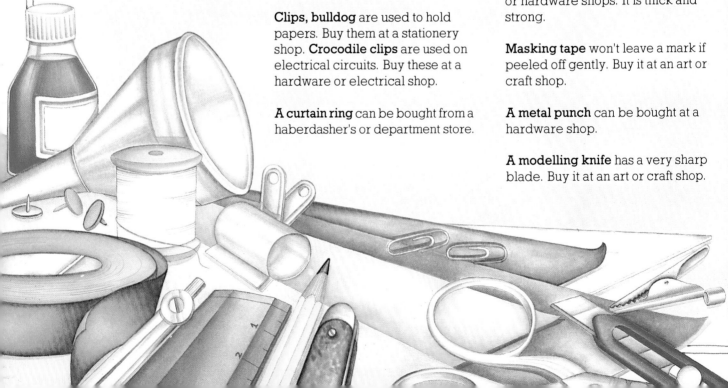

Nails are sold at hardware shops.

Nylon cord can be bought from sports' and camping shops, and some department stores.

Nylon fishing line can be bought from some sports' shops or a shop that sells fishing tackle.

Paper is sold at stationery shops and at art or craft shops. **A4 paper** (21cm × 29.5cm) is used by typists. You can use grease-proof paper instead of **tracing paper**.

Polythene is sold at hardware shops.

Potash alum crystals can be bought from a chemist or the science section of a large toy shop. Wash your hands after touching them.

A skewer is a metal spike often used to test cooked foods.

Sodium bicarbonate is used in cake-making. Buy it at a grocery shop or supermarket.

Spirit-based felt-tipped pens have ink that will not dissolve in water. Buy them at an art or craft shop.

Tapers and spills are used for testing gases. Tapers are made of wax, and spills of wood. Buy them from a tobacconist, a chemist or the science section of a large toy shop.

Test tubes can be bought from a chemist or the science section of a large toy shop.

Tubes, rubber, plastic and glass can be bought from shops that sell wine-making equipment, from some garden centres, or the science section of a large toy shop.

Wire is sold at hardware shops.

Laboratory procedure

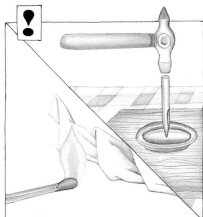

1. The exclamation symbol means that a tool (such as a metal punch) or a process (such as burning paper) can be dangerous. If you see this symbol on any part of an experiment, always ask an adult to read through the experiment with you before you start.

2. Put on old clothes, an overall or apron before starting.

3. Read through an experiment, then collect the materials listed.

4. Clear a work area and cover it with newspaper or other paper. Put an old wooden chopping board or cork tile on the work area if you have to cut anything.

5. Take care not to get anything in or near your eyes. If this happens, immediately rinse your eyes in clean water, and tell an adult.

6. Never eat or drink anything unless told you may do so in an experiment.

7. Clean up any mess you make.

8. Wash your hands if you have touched a chemical, and after you have finished an experiment.

Drawing a circle

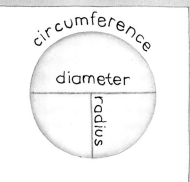

The radius is the distance between the centre of the circle and the circumference.
The diameter is double the radius.

1. Set the points of a pencil and a pair of compasses to the radius you require.

2. Put the point of the compasses firmly on a sheet of paper. It will mark the centre of the circle.

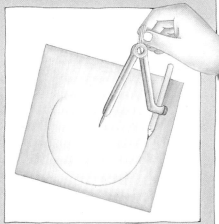

3. Swing the pencil round so that it draws a complete circle.

Vital air

Air is a mixture of invisible gases which are essential to life on earth. About four-fifths of the air consists of nitrogen, which is vital to plants. Oxygen, and a little carbon dioxide, make up most of the rest of the air. People and animals live by breathing oxygen. Plants, which are the only living things that can actually make oxygen, live by absorbing carbon dioxide. The experiments in this chapter show some characteristics of these essential gases.

Life-giving plants

This experiment proves that plants make oxygen.

Materials
- handful of pondweed or water-cress
- large, glass bowl or jar
- small, glass funnel and plasticine
- large jug of water
- small test tube
- matches and taper or spill

1. Put the pondweed into the bowl.

2. Upend the funnel over the weed, supporting it on blobs of plasticine about 2cm thick.

3. Add water to the bowl until the funnel is completely covered.

4. Fill the test tube with water.

5. Hold the index finger of your spare hand over the top of the tube.

6. Turn the tube upside down over the funnel, removing your finger when the tube is under water. Put the bowl on a sunny window sill or near a bright light for a few days.

7. When gas bubbles fill the tube, lift it off the funnel, covering the top with an index finger as you do so. Don't let any gas escape.

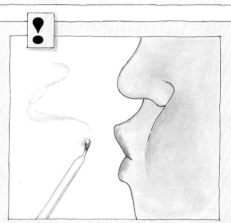

8. Ask someone to light the taper for you, then blow it out to get a glowing end.

9. Remove you finger and plunge the taper into the test tube. Don't let it touch the wet sides.

The taper will glow more brightly, or even relight. This shows that the gas made by the pondweed is oxygen, because oxygen supports burning.

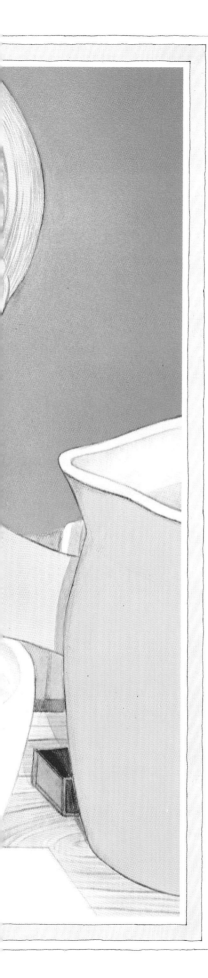

10

 # Electrolysis

Water consists of two parts hydrogen gas combined with one part oxygen. That's why its chemical formula is H_2O. Plants split up water by using energy from sunlight. You can do the same, using a battery for energy. Splitting up water by passing electricity through it is called electrolysis. Ask an adult to help you, and use a battery only. Do not try to use mains electricity, as it is extremely dangerous.

Materials
- empty washing-up liquid bottle
- modelling knife and scissors
- medium-sized cork soaked in cup of water
- 2 thick nails, each 10cm long
- about 50cm standard 1-core plastic-covered flex
- 4 small crocodile or bulldog clips
- small screwdriver
- 6 volt battery with terminals
- 300 ml water and 100 ml vinegar in jug
- 2 test tubes, each 9cm long
- matches and taper or spill

1. Cut the washing-up liquid bottle in half.

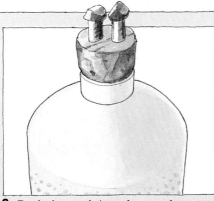

6. Push the cork into the nozzle opening.

7. Use scissors to cut the flex in half.

8. Strip about 2cm of plastic from each end of both lengths of flex. You will find lots of strands of shiny wire underneath.

9. Twist these fine strands into a single strand at each end.

10. Loosen the screws on each of the four crocodile clips.

11. Now fix one clip to each end of both lengths of flex by twisting the single strands of wire round the screws of the clips.

12. Use the screwdriver to tighten all the screws on the clips.

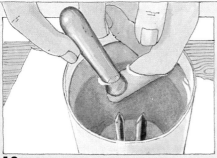

18. Fill one test tube with vinegar and water, hold an index finger over its top, and lower it over one nail.

19. Repeat step 18, using the other test tube and nail.

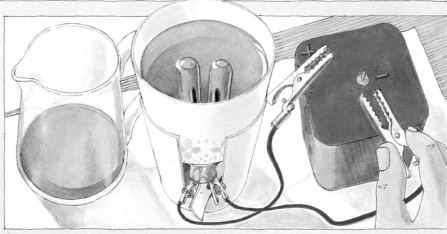

20. Attach one wire, using the clip, to the positive (+) terminal of the battery. Then attach the other wire to the negative (−) terminal in the same way.

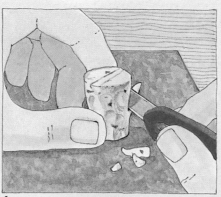

2. Cut (or pull) off the nozzle.

3. Thoroughly wash the two halves, then put the bottom half aside.

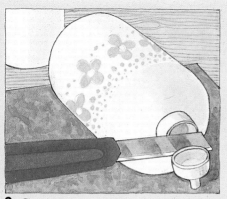

4. Trim the soaked cork so that it fits snugly into the nozzle opening. Remove the cork.

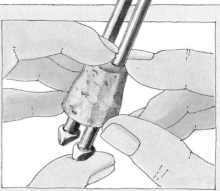

5. Ask someone to help you push the nails into the cork. They should not touch each other, and about 1cm of their heads should be left showing.

13. Clip one single strand of wire to the head of one nail and one to the head of the other nail.

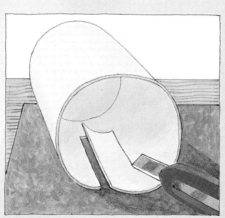

14. Cut out a wide slot in the side of the bottom half of the bottle.

15. Trim the cut-out strip and push it between the nails to make sure that they are separated.

16. Rest the top half of the bottle upside down in the bottom half, so that each length of flex with a clip on the end, runs through the slot.

17. Pour enough vinegar and water into the bottle to cover the nails by about 2cm.

21. In about 20 minutes, lift off the tube over the nail connected to the negative terminal, keeping a finger over the open end.

22. Ask someone to light the taper.

23. Remove your finger as the taper is held over the tube.

You will hear a squeaking pop, the sound hydrogen makes as it burns.

24. In about two hours, lift off the other tube, keeping a finger over it.

25. Ask someone to light the taper again, but to blow it out to get a glowing end.

26. Remove your finger as the taper is put into the tube.

The gas produced at the positive terminal gives quite a different reaction! You'll recognise it, if you have done the 'Life-giving plants' experiment on pp.8-9.

Nitrogen nodules

Air, which consists of about four-fifths nitrogen gas, also exists in soil. This experiment shows how beans produce lumps (or nodules) to help them convert nitrogen into food.

Materials

- small, glass jar
- damp garden soil and old spoon
- 3 or 4 runner bean seeds
- plastic bag and elastic band
- water

1. Put a layer of soil, about 4cm deep, into the jar.

2. Push the bean seeds between the soil and the side of the jar.

3. Cover the jar with the plastic bag, fixing it in place with the elastic band.

4. Put the jar in a warm, dark place, such as an airing cupboard, for about a week.

5. Look at the beans to see if they have germinated, or grown shoots. You should see a shoot and a white root. If not, put the jar back into the cupboard for a few more days.

6. Then uncover the jar and put it in the light for another week. Keep the soil moist.

The nodules that form on the roots of the beans are full of useful germs, or bacteria. These convert nitrogen into a form which the plant can absorb, then use to make protein, an essential part of our diet. Only vegetables of the bean and pea family can do this.

Secret messages

This experiment depends on heat to speed up oxidation. Oxidation is the reaction between a certain substance – in this case, potash alum crystals – and oxygen in the air. Wash your hands if you touch the crystals or the solution.

Materials

- 1 teaspoon potash alum crystals
- shallow saucer of water
- paint brush
- sheet of writing paper
- hot iron and ironing cloth

1. Mix the potash alum crystals with the water in the saucer to dissolve them.

2. Dip the paint brush into this mixture and write on the paper. Let the 'ink' dry.

3. Run a hot iron over the paper.

This special "ink" oxidizes at a lowe[r] temperature tha[n] paper, so it is affected more rapidly by the he[at]

Fruity oxidation

See how different fruits react with oxygen in the air, and enjoy a delicious dessert at the same time!

Materials

- ½ lemon and lemon squeezer
- small, glass bowl and saucer
- chopping board and table knife
- 1 apple, 1 banana and 1 peach
- 1 tablespoon sugar
- cling film
- cream (optional)

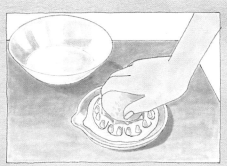

1. Squeeze the juice from the lemon and pour it into the bowl.

2. Cut the apple into quarters and cut out the core.

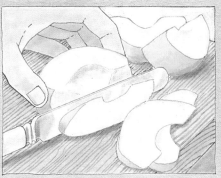

3. Slice the apple thinly.

4. Put one slice on the saucer and the rest into the bowl.

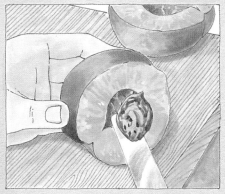

5. Halve the peach, cut out the stone and slice the fruit.

6. Repeat step 4.

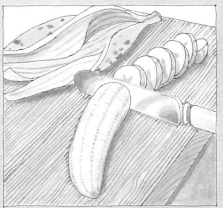

7. Peel and slice the banana.

8. Repeat step 4.

9. Add the sugar to the fruit salad and stir the mixture well.

10. Cover the bowl with cling film and put it into the refrigerator for about one hour.

11. Leave the saucer of fruit for one hour. Look at it often.

Some fruits oxidize when they are cut and exposed to air. The brown marks show that oxidation is taking place. Which fruit reacts fastest?

The fruit salad in the refrigerator won't go brown because coldness slows down oxidation. The vitamin C in lemon juice also helps prevent oxidation.

12. Pour cream on your fruit salad, if you like, and eat it for supper.

Bubble power

Carbon dioxide is the gas that people and animals breathe out. It may not seem very powerful, but this experiment proves otherwise!

Materials
- large, plastic bottle with cork
- 1 teaspoon sodium bicarbonate
- ¼ cup vinegar
- washing-up bowl

1. Put the sodium bicarbonate into the bottle.

2. Stand the bottle in the washing-up bowl.

3. Add the vinegar and quickly press in the cork. Stand well back!

The chemical reaction between sodium bicarbonate and vinegar produces carbon dioxide. The gas builds up pressure below the cork. Something must give way!

Fire extinguisher

Unlike oxygen, carbon dioxide will not burn. In fact, a foamy form of carbon dioxide is used to put out fires. Try mixing your own foamy carbon dioxide for this model fire extinguisher. It will look exactly like the real thing!

Materials
- about 25cm lightweight wire
- about 25cm rubber tube
- plastic bottle of about 500 ml capacity
- one-holed rubber bung to fit neck of bottle, or cork to fit neck of bottle, a skewer and penknife
- plasticine and eye-dropper
- 2 paper handkerchiefs
- 2 teaspoons sodium bicarbonate
- 50cm cotton thread and scissors
- 100 ml vinegar
- jug of water
- 3 teaspoons washing-up liquid

1. Push the wire into the rubber tube, leaving about 1cm extending from one end.

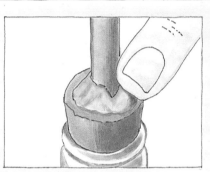

6. Use plasticine to seal round the tube and bung (or cork).

7. Pull the rubber teat off the eye-dropper. (You can push it back on when you have finished.)

8. Bend the spare end of the rubber tube into an arch, and push the jet of the eye-dropper on to it.

14. Take all the apparatus to the sink.

15. Put the vinegar into the bottle, then add water until the bottle is three-quarters full.

16. Add the washing-up liquid.

17. Practise moving the bung (or cork) in and out of the neck. You must be able to put it in smoothly and quickly in step 19.

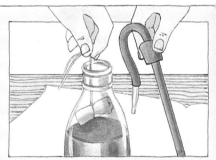

18. Lower the parcel into the bottle by its long threads, and hold it just above the liquid.

19. Let the parcel drop into the bottle, then quickly push the bung (or cork) into its neck.

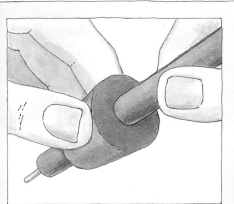

2. Push the tube, wire end first, into the hole in the rubber bung.

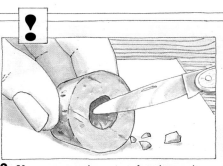

3. If you are using a cork, pierce it with the skewer and widen the hole with the penknife until the tube fits into the hole.

4. Push the bung (or cork) into the neck of the bottle.

5. Gently push down the tube until it almost touches the bottom of the bottle.

9. Remove the bung (or cork), being very careful not to disturb the plasticine round the tube. Put this part of the apparatus near the sink.

10. Lay one paper handkerchief on top of the other.

11. Put the sodium bicarbonate on the uppermost handkerchief.

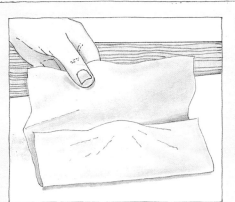

12. Fold over two opposite edges of the handkerchiefs, then roll them up into a very small parcel.

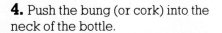

13. Tie up the parcel, leaving long ends of thread.

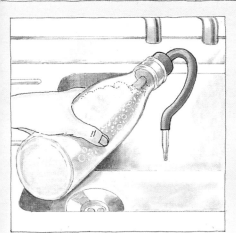

20. Shake the bottle, pointing the eye-dropper jet into the sink.

The sodium bicarbonate and vinegar react to form bubbles of carbon dioxide gas, and the gas is made foamy by the washing-up liquid. (Wash the eye-dropper jet when you have finished.)

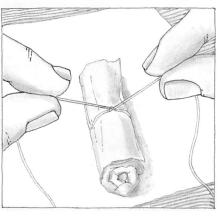

Fire!
You often see red cylinders labelled 'Fire extinguisher'. Inside these cylinders, there are chemicals which make carbon dioxide and then turn the gas into foam. The foam acts as a blanket, keeping air away from the fire. Without the oxygen in air to feed it, the fire will go out.

Watery air

You may be surprised to know that the air in your warm kitchen contains about two litres of water! This water is suspended invisibly in the air, in the form of gaseous water vapour. Water is drawn up into the air from rivers, seas and lakes, from small puddles and the tiniest leaves of plants. It becomes visible and falls back to earth as rain, hail or snow. The experiments in this chapter not only prove that water exists in air; they also show you some of the curious effects of 'watery air'.

Hygroscopic shortbread

Sugar is a hygroscopic substance, or one that absorbs moisture from the air. Hygroscopic means 'wet-looking'. Experiment to see what effect a hygroscopic substance has on a crisp biscuit which is left in the air. If you keep the rest of the biscuits in an air-tight container, you can eat them at tea-time.

Materials

- large mixing bowl
- 175 g plain flour
- ¼ teaspoon salt
- 50g castor sugar
- 125 g soft butter
- large, floured chopping board
- floured rolling pin
- floured table knife
- greased baking tray
- plate and air-tight container

1. Put the flour, salt and 40g of the sugar into the bowl.

2. Add the butter and mix the ingredients together with your hands until they form a firm ball.

3. Put the ball of mixture on the floured board and roll it out until it is about 1cm thick.

4. Set the oven to 170°C (325°F or gas mark 3).

5. Cut the mixture into about 16 small squares or rectangles.

6. Put the shapes on the greased baking tray and sprinkle them with the left-over 10g of sugar.

7. Put the tray into the oven for about 20 minutes, then take it out and let the biscuits cool.

8. Store all but one biscuit in the air-tight container.

9. Put one biscuit on the plate and leave it in the air overnight.

10. The next day, take a bite from the biscuit on the plate and a bite from one of the biscuits in the container. Which is crisper?

Making ice

Water vapour exists in the air in the form of an invisible gas. When the air is cold enough, this gas turns to liquid rain or even to solid hail, ice and snow. This experiment gives you instant 'winter'.

Materials

- clean, dry glass
- 3 ice cubes
- 3 tablespoons salt

1. Put the ice cubes and salt into the glass.

This forms a very cold mixture.

2. Watch the glass closely.

The outside of the glass will become wet because the coldness has turned the invisible moisture in the air into water. If you leave the glass a little longer, the water may turn to ice or the glass may freeze to the surface on which it is resting.

Noisy fir cones

If the weather is damp, fir cones keep their scales tightly closed to protect their seeds. But when the air is dry, the scales spring open to release their seeds. Sometimes, this action causes a loud, cracking noise.

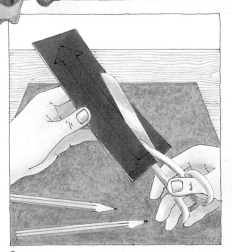

Hygrometer

A hygrometer is an instrument used to measure the amount of water in the air. Here's how to make a simple one using a human hair. Your hair absorbs moisture, and so lengthens on damp, humid days. On dry days, it 'shrinks', and so becomes shorter.

Materials

- tracing paper 6cm × 20cm
- soft (2B) and hard (3H) pencils
- white, or coloured, lightweight card 6cm × 20cm
- white, or coloured, stiff card about 22cm × 30cm
- scissors and sticky tape
- hair about 20cm long
- block of wood about 22cm × 4cm square
- drawing pins
- fine felt-tipped pen

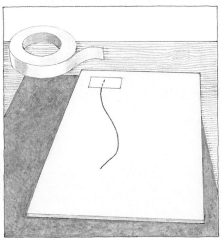

6. Cut out the cardboard arrow.

7. Stick one end of the hair to the top of the stiff card.

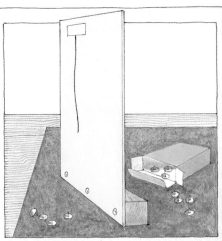

8. Use drawing pins to fix the card to one long edge of the block of wood, as shown.

Watery plants

Plants draw up their water from the soil, and lose it to the air through tiny holes in their leaves. This process is called transpiration, and you can see it at work in this experiment.

Materials
- house plant such as geranium
- large plastic bag
- string and scissors
- jug of water

1. Put the plastic bag over the plant.

2. Close the bag round the stem of the plant, and keep it closed by tying string round it.

3. Water the soil round the plant.

4. Put the plant outdoors in the sun.

After two or three hours, the inside of the bag will be covered with beads of moisture. Imagine how much water a tree loses to the air!

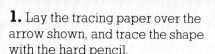

1. Lay the tracing paper over the arrow shown, and trace the shape with the hard pencil.

2. Take off the tracing paper and turn it over.

3. Shade across all the lines with the soft pencil.

4. Lay the tracing paper, shaded side down, on the lightweight card.

5. Draw over the lines with the hard pencil, then remove the paper.

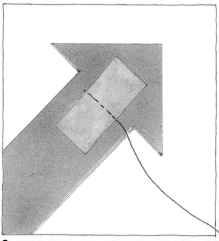

9. Stick the other end of the hair to the back of the head of the arrow.

10. Holding the arrow against the card, gently stretch the hair to its full length. Push a drawing pin through the blunt end of the arrow and into the stiff card.

11. Put the hygrometer outdoors.

12. On a sunny day, mark where the arrow rests and write 'dry' against this point. Write 'moist' against the lowest point the arrow reaches on a damp day. (Don't leave your hygrometer outdoors in the rain!)

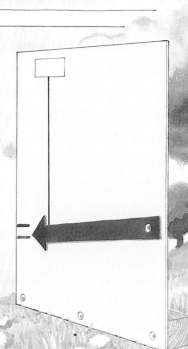

Dirty air

If no people lived on earth, the air would be much cleaner. We pollute the air, or make it dirty and unhealthy, by burning fuels in our factories, homes, cars and aeroplanes. People contribute far more to making air dirty than the volcanoes that throw out dust and ash or the bacteria that live in the air do. The experiments in this chapter will give you some idea of the importance of clean air and healthy lungs.

Making smog

Smog is a mixture of dirt, smoke, fumes and tiny drops of water, and is very bad for our health. In this experiment, you will see how such dirty air is formed.

Materials
- large, glass jar or bowl
- aluminium foil and scissors
- 3 to 5 ice cubes
- ruler and pencil
- salt
- twist of paper and matches

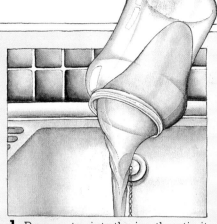

1. Pour water into the jar, then tip it out again.

The tiny drops of water left will make the air inside the jar damp.

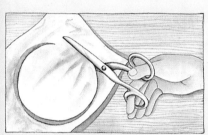

2. Cut out a circle of foil about 2cm larger than the neck of the jar.

3. Put the ice cubes on the foil and sprinkle salt over them.

4. Ask an adult to light the paper and drop it into the jar.

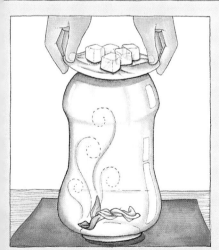

5. Quickly put the foil and ice cubes on top of the jar and press the foil to the sides.

Smoke and other gases rise upwards into the cold air of the earth's atmosphere. But if there is a layer of warm air below the cold, smoke and fumes will be trapped in it. This happens in your jar, just as dirty smog is trapped by the layer of warm air over a city.

Lichens

Lichens can show how polluted air is because they are sensitive to it.

Shrubby lichens are very sensitive to pollution. They grow only where the air is very clean. They look like tiny bushes, with long, hairy stems, and are usually grey or green.

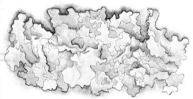

Leafy lichens can tolerate some pollution. Look for patches of flat, rounded, leaf-like shapes in grey, green, yellow, orange or black. The cleaner the air, the higher up on a tree or building this kind grows.

Crusty lichens are the most tolerant of pollution. Look for them low down on trees growing in town centres, and higher up on trees growing on the outskirts of towns. These lichens form flat, crazy-paving patterns, and are often green or grey.

Smoking machine

You'll believe that it's dangerous to smoke when you see the amount of tar in a cigarette! This kind of dirty 'air' makes healthy, pink lungs horribly black. Ask an adult to do this experiment with you.

Materials
- empty washing-up liquid bottle
- modelling knife
- 10cm plastic or glass tube about 1cm in diameter
- small piece of cotton wool
- skewer or length of wire
- masking or insulating tape
- scissors
- filter cigarette and matches
- ashtray

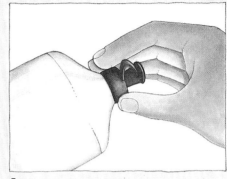

1. Pull (or cut) off the nozzle of the washing-up liquid bottle.

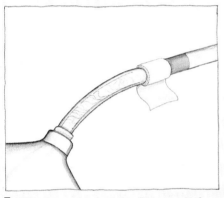

5. Wind tape round the filter end of the cigarette and the end of the tube to seal them together.

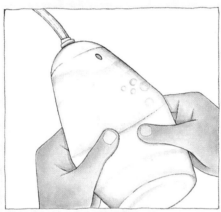

6. Squeeze the washing-up liquid bottle to push out some of the air.

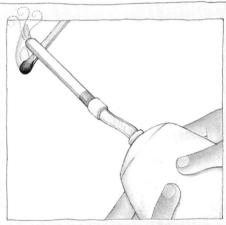

7. Cover the hole with your thumb while an adult lights the cigarette.

Breath power

Ask a friend to help you do this breathing experiment. You'll see why smokers are at a disadvantage when they do any exercise. You need quite a lot of oxygen to do even a little exercise. Smokers get 'out of breath' because tar clogs up their lungs.

Materials
- watch or clock with second hand
- pencil and sheet of writing paper

1. Ask your friend to lie on the floor.

2. Count how many times your friend's chest or stomach rises and falls in one minute.

normal 18

after 3 minutes

3. Note the figure, and count again after your friend has been lying quietly for three minutes.

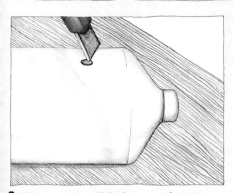

2. Pierce a small hole near the top of the bottle.

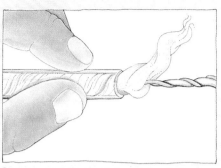

3. Use the skewer to poke a thin twist of cotton wool into the tube. Pack the wool loosely.

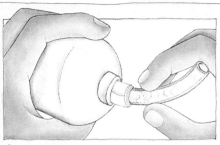

4. Push one end of the tube into the nozzle opening. If it does not fit snugly, take it out and wind some masking tape round it.

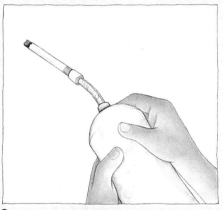

8. Keeping your thumb over the hole, press the bottle back to its full shape to draw in cigarette smoke.

9. Remove your thumb and squeeze the bottle to push out air again, as shown in step 6.

10. Holding the cigarette over the ashtray, repeat steps 8 and 9 until the cigarette has burned away.

11. Unwind the tape holding the cigarette and put the remains of the cigarette in the ashtray.

12. Pull the tube out of the nozzle.

13. Gently push out the cotton wool, using the skewer.

The cotton wool will be covered in tar. You will also note the horrible smell!

4. Ask your friend to run up and down stairs, or round the room, and then to lie on the floor again while you take another count.

5. Compare the three figures.

When we take a breath, we draw in all the gases present in the air. But the only one we make use of is oxygen, which passes from the lungs into the blood. The more energy that you produce, the more air you need.

Mighty lungs

This experiment tests lung capacity. If you could spread out your lungs completely flat, they would be about as big as a tennis court. But their effective size is reduced by smoking, or by breathing dirty air.

Materials

- masking tape and scissors
- clear plastic container of about 5 litre capacity
- 60cm rubber or plastic tube
- spirit-based felt-tipped pen
- measuring jug

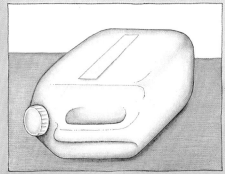

1. Stick a strip of masking tape down the length of the container.

2. Fill the bath with water.

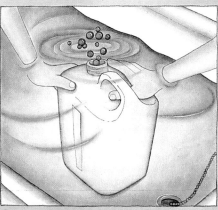

3. Put the container under the water so that it fills up.

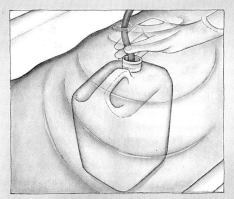

4. Slide one end of the tube into the container. The other end should be above the surface of the water.

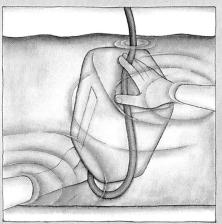

5. Turn the container upside down under the water.

6. Holding the container steady, take a deep breath and blow into the tube for as long as possible.

The air going into the container will force out the water.

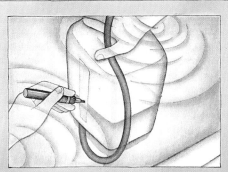

7. Mark the level of the water left in the container.

8. Empty the container and lift it out of the bath.

9. Pour water from the measuring jug into the container, up to the level marked on the masking tape.

10. Note the amount of water you have poured into the container.

This is the same as the amount of air your lungs can hold.

You could ask some friends to do this experiment, and compare their lung capacities with yours.

Gravy horror

Bacteria, or germs, are tiny forms of life that multiply if they are kept warm and fed. They are always present in the air, although you cannot see them. Some bacteria are useful to us and some are not. But they make interesting subjects for experiment!

Materials

- 3 clean, glass jars, 2 with lids
- metal punch and hammer
- warm, meaty gravy or stew
- 3 sticky labels and pen
- plastic or plastic-coated straw
- 30cm rubber tube
- 30cm lightweight wire
- plasticine

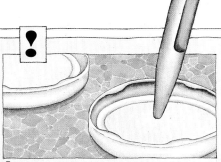

1. Ask an adult to punch a hole in each lid. The straw should be able to fit into one hole, and the tube into the other.

2. Half-fill each jar with the meaty gravy (or stew).

3. Label the jars '1', '2' and '3'. Put jar '1' aside.

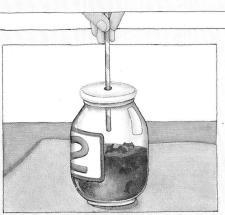

4. Screw a lid on to jar '2' and push the straw through the hole until it almost touches the gravy.

5. Push the wire through the rubber tube. This makes it pliable.

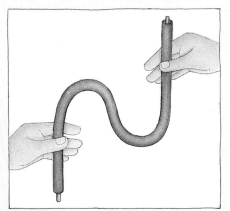

6. Bend the tube into an 's'-shape, making sure it has no kinks in it.

7. Screw a lid on to jar '3'.

8. Push one end of the 's'-shaped tube through the lid until it almost touches the gravy.

9. Seal any gaps with plasticine.

10. Put all three jars in a warm place for three or four days. A garden shed or garage is ideal, as the gravies will soon smell awful!

The gravy in jar '3' will not go bad as rapidly as the other gravies, because germs cannot travel round the bend to reach it. But you'll see some amazing changes in all three jars as the bacteria get to work. Do not taste any of the gravies, and pour them down the drain when you have finished.

Air pressure

Air has weight and so exerts pressure. The air in a room can weigh as much as 100 kg – about the same as a large person. Air can also be squeezed, or compressed, into small containers. Underwater divers breathe air that has been compressed into small cylinders. When you do the experiments in this chapter, you will see how amazingly powerful air is!

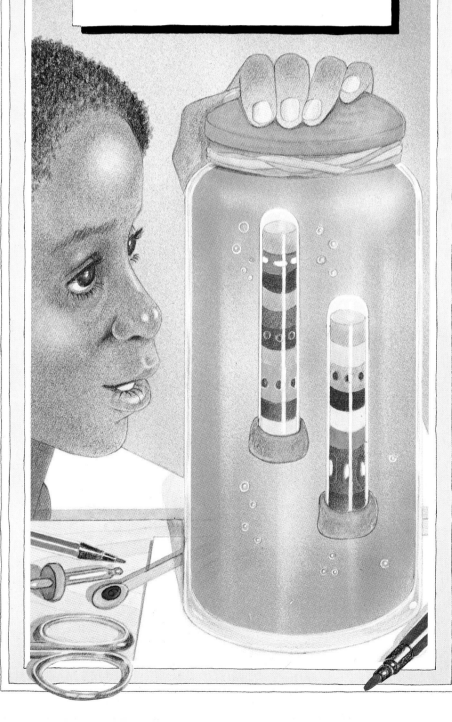

Diving bell

This toy will rise and fall exactly as a diving bell does. Diving machines that move by using air pressure are often described as 'Cartesian', because the principle was explained by René Descartes, a 16th-century French mathematician.

3. Stretch the balloon tightly over the neck of the jar and hold it in place with the elastic band. The balloon should spring back when you press down on it with your fingers. Take off the balloon and elastic band and put them aside.

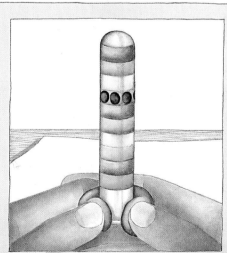

8. Roll the plasticine into a fat sausage-shape and press it round the upside-down tube.

Materials

- tall, glass jar almost filled with water
- blue food dye and eye-dropper
- large balloon and scissors
- large elastic band
- test tube about 10cm long
- writing paper about 3.5cm × 7cm
- felt-tipped pens
- small ball of plasticine
- knitting needle

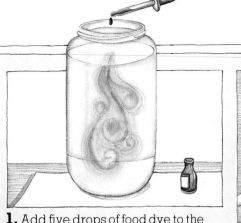

1. Add five drops of food dye to the water in the jar.

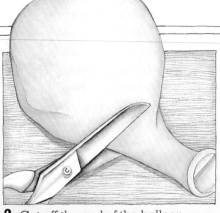

2. Cut off the end of the balloon.

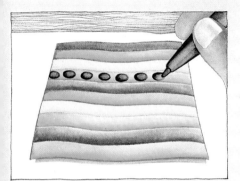

4. Draw 'portholes' on the paper.

5. Trim the paper if necessary. It must be about 1.5cm shorter than the tube, and wide enough to be rolled up and slipped inside it.

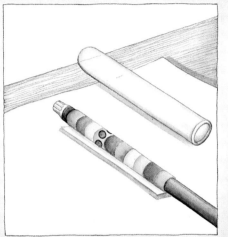

6. Roll the paper round a pen. (Hold it in place with your thumb.)

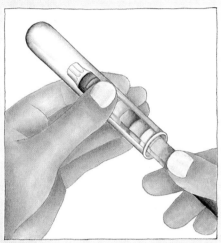

7. Push the pen half-way into the tube, then release the paper.

9. Drop the model into the jar.

It should sink, then rise again until its head is just above the surface of the water.
If the bell stays on the bottom, use the knitting needle to stab into the plasticine and lift out the bell. Pinch off a little plasticine.
If the head of the model shows well above the surface of the water, press on more plasticine.

10. Fix the balloon over the neck of the jar as shown in step 3.

11. Put your fingers on the balloon and press down until the bell sinks to the bottom of the jar.

12. Release your fingers to make the diving bell rise again.

The pressure of your fingers on the balloon is carried, by the water, to the air in the test tube. This squeezes the air, and water enters the test tube, making it sink.

Happy diving!

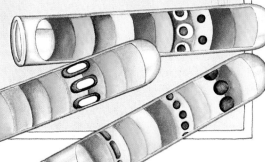

Easy pour

Next time someone is about to open a tin of milk or fruit juice, ask to see what happens if only one hole is punched in the top of the tin. Air pressure pushes on the liquid, holding it in. But if two holes are punched, more air can flow into the tin and so the liquid will escape easily.

Watering can

Did you know that air pressure can help you look after your plants? Prove it by making this little watering can from an empty tin. Use it to water garden or window box plants. It has too wide a sprinkling range for indoor use.

Materials
- small, metal tin with press-on lid
- metal punch and hammer
- newspaper
- enamel paint and paint brush
- water-proof transfers (optional)
- bowl of water

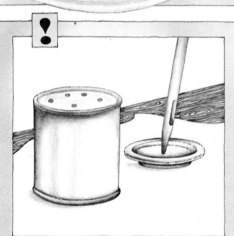

1. Ask an adult to punch five or six small holes in the bottom of the tin, and one small hole in the lid.

2. Paint the tin and lid. Don't block up the holes with paint.
Let the paint dry.

3. Decorate the tin with transfers, if you like.

4. Take the tin and the bowl of water outdoors.

5. Completely submerge the tin in the bowl of water.

Water will flow in through the holes in the bottom of the tin, forcing air out through the hole in the lid.

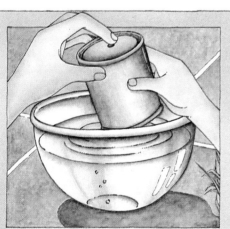

6. When the tin is full, put one finger over the hole in the lid and lift up the tin with your other hand.

Air pressing up on the bottom of the tin will hold the water inside.

7. Hold your watering can over some thirsty plants, and lift your finger.

As the air goes into the can, the water will come sprinkling out.

Exploding egg

This is a very dramatic experiment!
If you use a narrow-necked bottle,
your egg will be really pulverised.
You'll have to feed it to a pet when
you have finished the experiment!

Materials
- raw egg
- saucepan of boiling water
- narrow-necked, glass bottle
- twist of paper
- matches

1. Boil the egg for 10 minutes.
Let it cool.

2. Peel off the egg-shell.

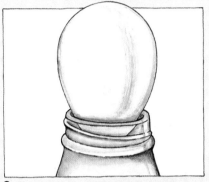

3. Rest the egg, pointed end down,
in the neck of the bottle.

The egg stays there because the
pressure inside and outside the
bottle are exactly the same.

4. Lift off the egg and hold it.

5. Ask an adult to light the twist of
paper and drop it into the bottle.
Quickly rest the egg in the neck of
the bottle, as shown in step 3.

Burning heats the air in the bottle.
The hot air expands and rises,
forcing its way out of the bottle. As
the bottle cools, the air contracts.
Air pressure outside the bottle is
now greater than that inside, and so
the egg is forced downwards.
Watch the explosion!

Topsy-turvy water

Show your friends and family how
to turn a glass of water upside down
without letting the water fall out.
This is an easy trick, but practise
over the sink first.

Materials
- glass with smooth rim
- stiff card about 6cm square
- water

1. Fill the glass to the very top with
water.

2. Hold the card firmly on the rim.

3. Keeping one hand on the card,
gently turn the glass upside down.

4. Slowly take away the hand
holding the card.

The card, held up by air pressure,
keeps the water from falling out of
the glass. Air exerts pressure from
all directions. In fact, air could hold
up a 10m-high column of water!

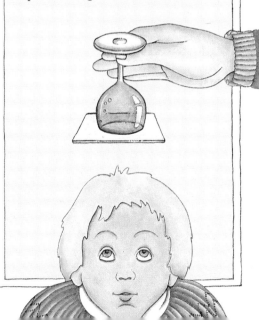

Siphon

You can use a siphon for many purposes, including emptying a fish tank before cleaning it. (Don't forget to take out the fish first!)

Materials
- bowl half-full of water
- short, rubber tube
- 2 glasses, each half-full of water

1. Hold each end of the tube and put both ends underwater in the bowl.

The tube will fill with water.

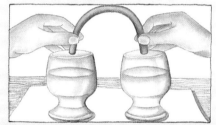

2. Pinch the ends of the tube to hold in the water, then put the ends underwater in separate glasses.

3. Release the ends of the tube.

4. Gently holding the tube, lift one glass higher than the other.

The water will flow from the higher glass to the lower one.

5. Before the higher glass is empty, lower it below the other glass.

The water will keep on flowing from the higher glass.

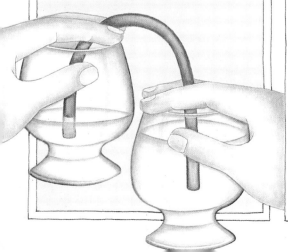

Noisy air

Air can be squeezed, or compressed. Letting it expand again enables it to do some powerful jobs. The brakes on many big lorries work on compressed air. The loud hissing noise is made by the air which escapes as the driver releases the brakes.

Hovercraft

A hovercraft floats on a cushion of compressed air, which is trapped beneath its 'skirt'. Propellers enable the hovercraft to move backwards and forwards, and powerful fans keep pumping air under the skirt. You can make a model hovercraft which will move on a smooth, flat surface.

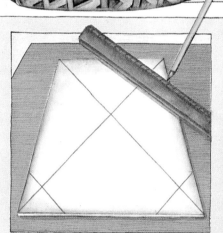

3. Join these points by drawing lines across each corner.

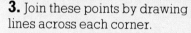

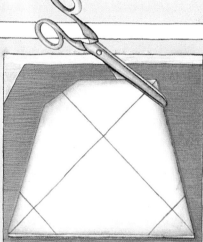

4. Cut off these corners.

9. Roll the 4cm × 19cm strip of card into a tube and put it into the cut-out hole. It should fit snugly.

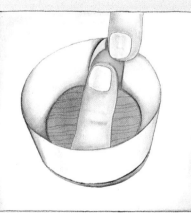

10. Join the inside edge of the tube with tape.

Materials

- lightweight card 18cm × 30cm
- lightweight card 4cm × 19cm
- 2 strips lightweight card, each 3cm × 35cm
- ruler and pencil
- penknife and scissors
- pair of compasses
- insulating or masking tape
- poster paint and paint brush

1. Draw two straight lines to join the opposite corners of the large sheet of card.

These lines are called diagonals, and the point where they cross is the centre of the card.

2. Measure and mark points 5cm from each corner.

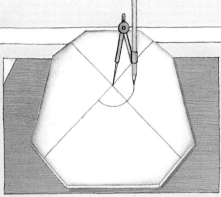

5. With the point of the compasses on the centre of the card, draw a 3cm-radius circle (see p.7).

6. Cut out the circle with the penknife. This completes the deck.

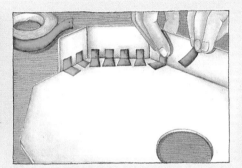

7. Use small pieces of tape to fix the two 3cm × 35cm strips to the bottom edge of the card. Overlap the ends of the strips. This forms the skirt.

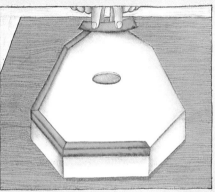

8. Turn the hovercraft over and put sticky tape along all the edges between the skirt and the deck.

11. Tape the tube to the underside of the deck.

12. Paint the hovercraft. Let the paint dry.

13. Put the hovercraft on a smooth, flat surface. Blow down the tube to make the craft move. Take a breath and blow again!

On a real hovercraft, the fans supply a constant stream of air.

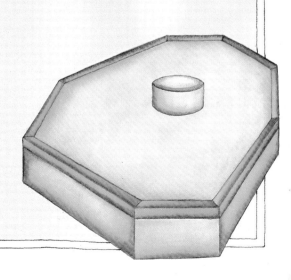

Light air

Although air has weight, we are not aware of it. Air and wind feel light when they touch your skin. But air actually becomes lighter, or less dense, when it is heated, and so it rises. Winds are caused by warm air rising and cold air moving in to take its place. This chapter shows some of the exciting uses of 'light' air.

Fan mobile

A mobile is designed to twirl in a rising current of warm air. Here's a simple, yet effective, mobile.

Materials
- 4 sheets lightweight, coloured paper, each 12cm square
- pair of compasses
- ruler, pencil and scissors
- sewing needle
- reel of cotton thread
- 32cm cane or bamboo stick
- masking tape

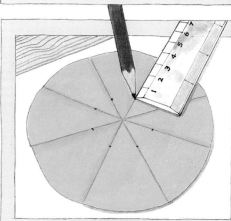

6. Measure and mark points 3.5cm from the edge on all eight fold lines of each circle.

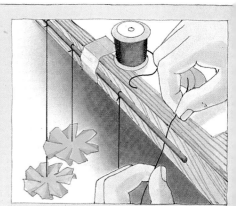

12. Tape the stick to a table edge and tie each fan to it so that they hang at different lengths.
Trim the knots and remove the tape.

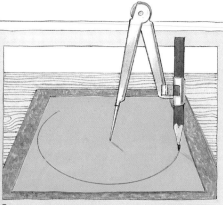

1. Use the compasses and pencil to draw a 5cm-radius circle (see p.7) on each sheet of paper.

2. Cut out the paper circles.

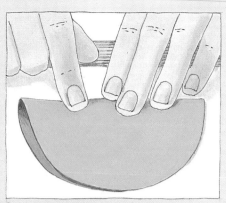

3. Fold each circle in half.

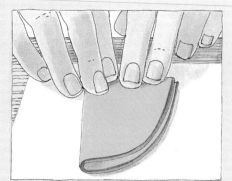

4. Fold each circle in half again, then in half once more.

5. Open out each circle.

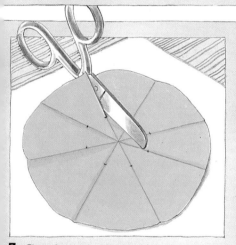

7. Cut along the fold lines to each mark.

8. Gently twist up the blades of each fan in the same direction.

9. Tie a knot in one end of 30cm of thread and thread the needle.

10. Push the needle through the middle of one fan and draw the thread through.
Remove the needle.

11. Repeat steps 9 and 10 to finish the other fans.

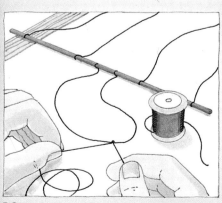

13. Tie the ends of 30cm of thread, 2cm apart, to the middle of the stick. Then tie 25cm of thread to the middle of the centre thread.

14. Ask an adult to find the best place for you to hang the mobile so that it is over a radiator or electric lamp. Don't hang the mobile near an open fire or flame.

The rising hot air will drive the fans continuously.

Hot-air power

Don't miss seeing a hot-air balloon race if you get the chance! Hot-air balloons look very beautiful floating in the sky. The air inside is heated by a gas flame below the balloon. The warm air rises and carries the balloon upwards. When the gas flame is lowered, the air cools, and the balloon sinks back to the earth.

Star mobile

Mobiles will twirl in the lightest breath of air, so you needn't always hang them over a rising current of warm air. This star design will turn very well if you suspend it near a window or doorway, where it can catch a gentle breeze.

Materials

- 5 sheets lightweight, coloured paper, each 15cm × 10cm
- ruler and pencil
- scissors
- clear sticky tape
- sewing needle
- reel of cotton thread
- masking tape
- 3 bamboo or cane sticks, two 15cm long and one 25cm long

1. On one sheet of paper, measure and mark points 1cm from one end.

2. Draw a straight line through these points.

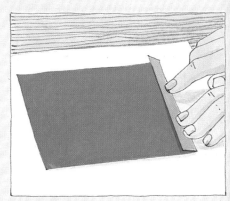

3. Fold the paper on this line.

7. Fold the strip of paper in half and cut across the ends.

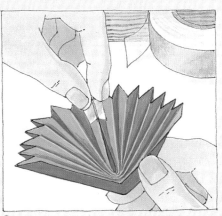

8. Fan out the star a little and use clear sticky tape to join two of the long edges.

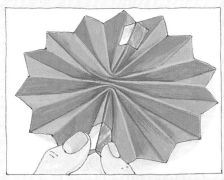

9. Gently fan out the rest of the star and tape the other two long edges together.

10. Tie a knot in one end of 40cm of thread and thread the needle.

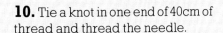

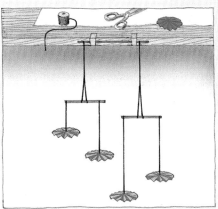

15. Tie the threads on the two short sticks to the ends of the long stick.

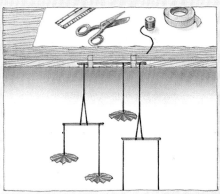

16. Tie the fifth star to the long stick so that it hangs above the short sticks.

17. Tie a hanging thread to the long stick, as shown in step 13 of 'Fan mobile' (see pp.32-33).

18. Hold the mobile so that it swings freely, and check the balance. If necessary, slide the thread of the stars to and fro until the mobile is perfectly balanced.

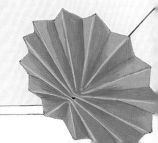

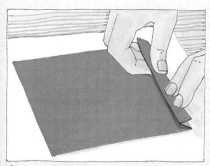

4. Turn the paper over and fold it up 1cm on this side.

5. Turn the paper over again and fold it up 1cm on this side.

6. Repeat steps 4 and 5 until the paper is completely folded into a 1cm-wide strip.

11. Push the needle and thread through the middle of the star. Remove the needle.

12. Repeat steps 1-11 to make four more stars.

13. Hang two stars to each short stick by following step 12 of 'Fan mobile' (see pp.32-33).
Then attach threads to the short sticks by following step 13 of the same experiment.

14. Tape the long stick to the edge of the table.

Wind sock

You may have seen wind socks at airports. They indicate the strength and direction of the wind, and so tell pilots at what speed they should land. This home-made 'sock' works on the same principle.

Materials
- old shirt-sleeve or stocking
- scissors
- 40cm lightweight, but firm, wire
- sewing needle
- cotton thread
- stone or weight
- 1m string

1. Cut the shirt-sleeve (or stocking) in half.

2. Bend the wire into a circle.

3. Pull one open end of the sleeve over the wire circle.

4. Sew the overlapping edges with a few stitches to hold it in place.

5. Sew the stone (or weight) into the sleeve near the wire circle.

6. Tie one end of the string to the circle, opposite the stone.

7. Tie the other end of the string to the branch of a tree. The stone will hold the mouth of the shirt-sleeve facing into the wind.

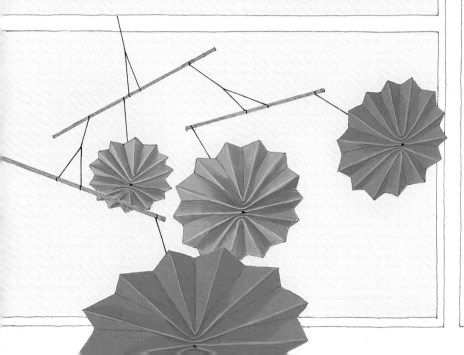

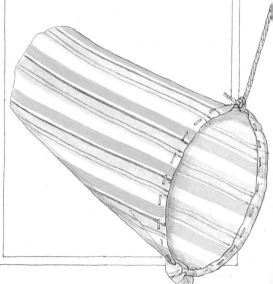

Flying seeds

You have probably played the game of blowing seeds off the heads of dandelions. Where those seeds settle, new plants will grow. Winds carry seeds to new ground, too. Autumn is the best time to look for seeds sailing through the air.

Windmill

People have been using windmills for over 4,000 years. Windmills can pump water, grind grain and generate electricity. This toy windmill works in exactly the same way – using the free energy of moving air.

Materials

- lightweight, coloured card or stiff paper 20cm square
- ruler, pencil and rubber
- scissors
- strong glue
- 60cm of 0.5cm dowelling
- drawing pin

1. Join the opposite corners of the card by drawing lines between them.

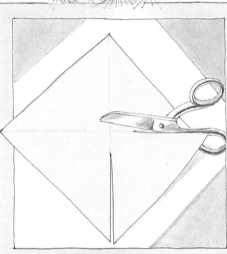

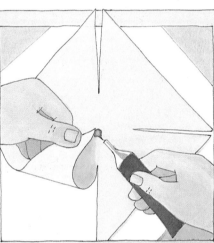

2. Cut about 10cm along the lines from each corner.

3. Rub out the pencil marks, leaving a dot to mark the centre.

4. Curl in one blade so that its tip is near the centre of the card, then glue the tip into place.

5. Repeat step 4 with all the blades. Let the glue dry.

6. Push the drawing pin through the centre of the card and into one end of the dowelling. The blades should be able to turn easily.

7. Hold the windmill in a light breeze, or swing it through the air.

The blades of your toy work in the same way as the giant sails of a real windmill.

Airy dessert

Some foods, such as meringues, souffles and mousses, are often said to be as 'light as air'. In fact, they are all made by whisking air into the ingredients. This makes the ingredients lighter and bigger. See how air can 'inflate' food by making this delicious dessert.

Materials
- 1 packet strawberry jelly
- hot and cold water
- jug and small bowl
- large tin of strawberries
- tin opener
- sieve and cup or bowl
- 2 large, deep, glass bowls
- 170 g evaporated milk
- rotary whisk and tablespoon

1. Make up the jelly with hot and cold water, following the instructions on the packet.

2. Pour the liquid jelly into the small bowl and put it into the refrigerator until it begins to set.

3. Take out the jelly when it is still wobbly.

4. Open the tin of strawberries and strain off the syrup.

5. Arrange the strawberries in a layer in the bottom of one deep bowl.
Put this bowl aside.

6. Pour the evaporated milk into the other deep bowl and whisk it vigorously.

You are whisking air into the milk, so it will increase in size.

7. When the milk is very thick and fluffy, whisk in a spoonful of jelly.

8. Keep adding and whisking until all the jelly has been used up.

9. Pour this fluffy mixture on top of the strawberries.

10. Put the dessert into the refrigerator and leave it for about two hours, or until it is set.

When you scoop out a spoonful of the dessert, you will see lots of tiny holes in it. These are bubbles of air, which help keep the dessert light and fluffy.

Aerodynamics

Aerodynamics deals with the science of moving through the air. Things that travel through air most easily are streamlined in shape. The more edges or angles on a flying object, the more resistance air can exert on it. The more air resistance it has, the more energy an object needs in order to move. Aerodynamics is an important science, and a lot of fun, as you will find out.

Outdoor rotor

This rotor resembles the boomerang that the Australian Aborigines have used for hunting and fighting since the Stone Age. Never throw a rotor at any person or animal.

Materials
- 2 pieces balsa wood, each 2.5cm × 15cm × 3mm
- small, strong elastic band
- soft (2B) pencil
- fine glasspaper and clean cloth
- balsa wood glue
- gloss paints and paint brush

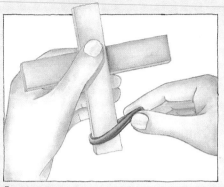

1. Hold the pieces of balsa wood across each other, and slip the elastic band over one end of the vertical arm.

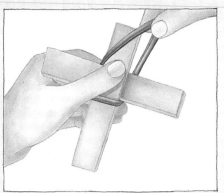

2. Pull the band up behind the horizontal arm, then loop it over the top of the vertical arm.

3. Move the horizontal arm about half-way down the vertical arm.

4. Choose a calm day to take the rotor outdoors to test it. Hold one tip of the rotor and face into any slight breeze. Lift the rotor up behind your head, then launch it as if you were serving at tennis. Try to spin it as you throw. You may need to adjust the arms of the rotor to find the best position for flight.

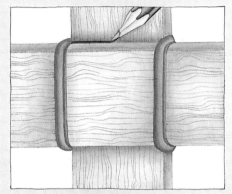

5. Mark the position of the horizontal arm on the vertical arm.

6. Take off the elastic band.

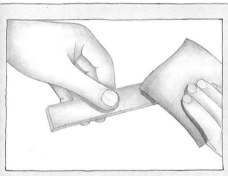

7. Gently rub glasspaper over the arms to make them smooth, missing out the pencilled area.

8. Wipe the wood with the cloth.

9. Glue the horizontal arm to the vertical arm between the two pencil marks. Let the glue dry.

10. Paint one side of the rotor. Let the paint dry.

11. Paint the other side of the rotor and let the paint dry.

When you are ready to demonstrate your throwing skill, use the same technique as described in step 4.

Indoor boomerang

Like the 'Outdoor rotor' (see pp.38-39), this boomerang has both lift and turning ability. As it is made of card, you can throw it indoors. You may need to practise the throwing, as there is a certain knack to it. Watch someone throwing a frisbee to see how it should be done.

Materials
- stiff card about 20cm square
- pair of compasses
- pencil and ruler
- modelling knife
- scissors

1. Use the compasses and pencil to draw a circle with a 9cm radius (see p.7) on the card.

2. With the point of the compasses on the centre of the card, draw a circle with a 2cm radius.

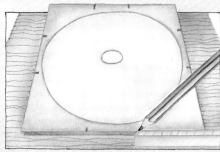

3. Measure and mark points 8cm from each corner.

4. Rule lines between the marks on opposite sides of the card.

Parachute

Air resistance can be very useful. A parachute, for instance, could not descend gently if air resistance did not slow it down. Five centuries ago, Leonardo da Vinci worked out many ideas for making parachutes. This is a model of one of them, so you are following in the tradition of a great scientist and inventor!

Materials
- heavy paper 30cm × 17cm
- ruler, pencil and scissors
- paper glue
- sewing needle
- four 20cm-lengths cotton thread, each knotted at one end
- empty match-box and plasticine
- clear sticky tape

1. Measure and mark points half-way across the paper.

2. Draw a straight line through the points to divide the paper in half.

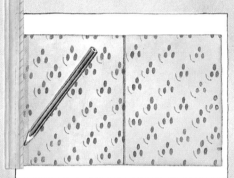

3. Mark points 2cm up from the bottom edge of the paper.

4. Draw a straight line through these points.

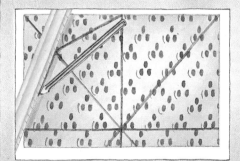

9. Continue this line from the same 15cm-mark to the end of the 2cm-line across the bottom of the paper.

10. Repeat steps 8 and 9, working on the right-hand side of the paper.

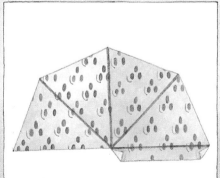

11. Cut out the areas shown and fold in the corners of the flap.

12. Fold the paper along all four pencilled lines, overlapping the edges and gluing them together. Let the glue dry.

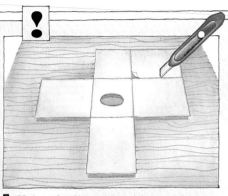

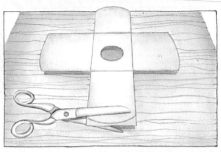

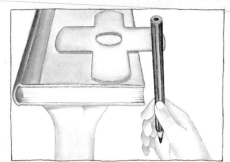

5. Using the lines as guides, cut out the corners and discard them. Cut out the central circle.

6. Use the scissors to round off each tip, then slightly bend up two opposite corners.

7. Lay the boomerang on a book or on your palm, as shown. Tap the tip sharply to make the model fly.

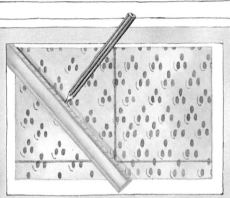

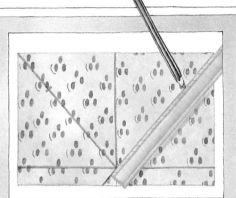

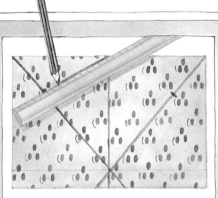

5. Draw a line from the top left-hand corner, through the point where the lines meet, to the bottom edge.

6. Repeat step 5 from the top right-hand corner.

7. Measuring from the point where all the lines meet, mark 15cm along the lines shown.

8. Draw a line from the middle of the top of the paper to the 15cm-mark on the left-hand side.

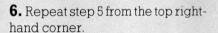

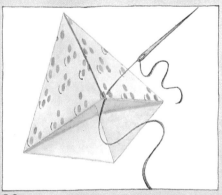

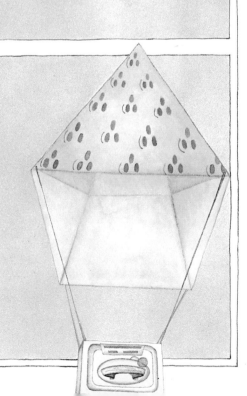

13. Thread the needle and push it and the thread through one corner of the parachute. Remove the needle.

14. Repeat step 13 on the other corners of the parachute.

15. Put some plasticine into the match-box.

16. Pull the ends of the threads together and tape them to the match-box.

17. Drop your parachute from the top of some stairs.

If it falls too quickly, take out a little plasticine. If it falls too slowly, increase the load.

Helicopter

The blades of this helicopter turn very fast, letting the model spin dramatically towards the floor. This happens because the helicopter blades have resistance to air.

Materials

- lightweight paper 6cm × 20cm
- pencil and ruler
- scissors
- paper clips

1. Measure and mark two points 9cm up from the bottom of the paper.

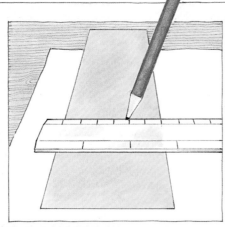

2. Draw a straight line between the points.

3. Measure and mark 2cm in from the edges along this line.

4. Mark 2cm in from each corner on the bottom of the paper.

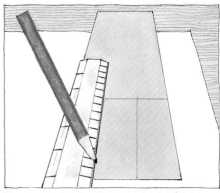

5. Draw straight lines between the opposite marks.

6. Cut out the areas shown.

7. Measure half-way across the top edge of the paper.

8. With the ruler parallel to the long sides, draw a straight line 9cm long from the half-way mark.

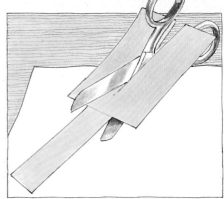

9. Cut from the top edge of the paper to the end of the 9cm-line.

10. Fold one blade towards you and the other away.

11. Fold up the bottom edge about 1cm and fix a paper clip to the fold.

12. Stand on some stairs and let the helicopter fall to the ground.

If you want to make a helicopter which falls more slowly, adjust the measurements to make wider blades. The wider the blade, the greater air resistance the helicopter has.

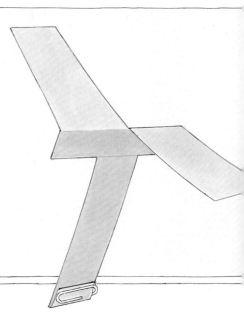

Paper Concorde

The shape of Concorde is a very streamlined one. You can see this by making a model to fly indoors.

Materials
- sheet of A4 paper (21cm × 29.5cm)
- 6cm masking tape
- scissors

1. Fold the paper in half lengthways.

2. Open it out, folded edge up.

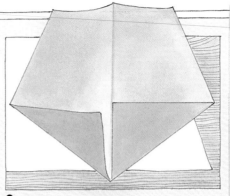

3. Fold in the top corners to meet the centre fold.

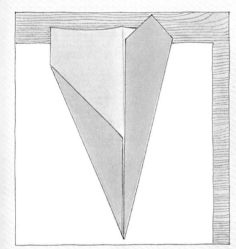

4. Fold these corners in again, then in once more.

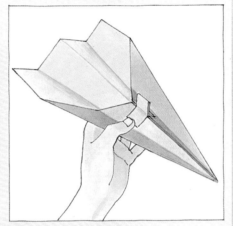

5. Stick the tape across the inner folds so that it joins them as well as forming a tab for you to hold.

6. Hold the folds together and cut off the tip of the tail.

7. Bend down the nose of the plane.

8. Hold the tab with one hand, and gently launch Concorde into the air.

Smooth shapes

Wherever you go take notice of the shape of things that travel through the air. They are designed to push air out of the way. The more streamlined the shape, the less resistance it has.

A supersonic jet is an efficient flying machine, with few angles to provide air resistance.

A racing car is low, with a small surface area and smooth lines.

A high-speed train has long, straight lines and a curved front which pushes air aside.

Even a bird has a streamlined shape. This helps it to save energy when it flies over long distances.

Flat kite

A kite is a perfect example of simple aerodynamic lift. Flying one takes some practise, but once you master the art, you can have hours of fun. A fabric or polythene kite will last a long time.

Materials

- two 70cm-lengths of 5mm dowelling
- tape measure
- soft (2B) pencil
- 100 cm nylon fishing line
- scissors
- 40m of 1mm nylon cord
- 4 drawing pins
- lightweight fabric 80cm square and fabric glue, or polythene 80cm square and clear sticky tape
- 14 strips coloured tissue paper, each 15cm × 30cm
- 15cm wooden stick
- curtain ring

1. Mark a point 20cm from one end of one length of dowelling. This length is the spine of the kite.

2. Mark 35cm from one end of the other length of dowelling (the spar).

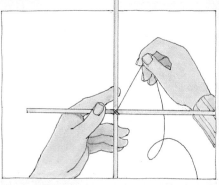

3. Put the spar across the spine on the marks, and wind the 100 cm of nylon fishing line crossways round the joint. Tie double knots.

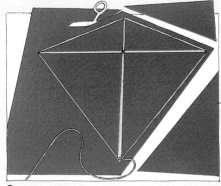

8. Lay the frame on the fabric (or polythene) and cut round the shape, leaving an extra 2cm.

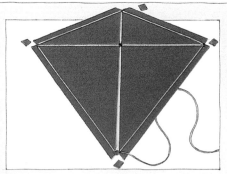
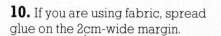

9. Cut 'v'-shapes out of each corner of the covering.

10. If you are using fabric, spread glue on the 2cm-wide margin.

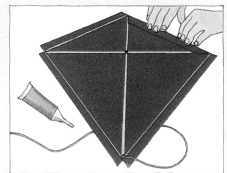

11. Pull the covering tight and fold over the gluey margin on the fabric. (Use sticky tape to fix polythene.)

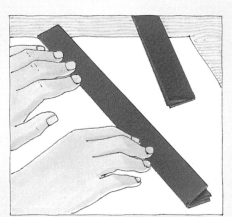

15. Fold the tissue paper strips in half lengthways, then in half again.

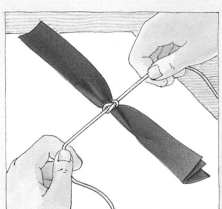

16. Tie and knot the tail of the kite round the middle of each strip. Space the strips about 15cm apart.

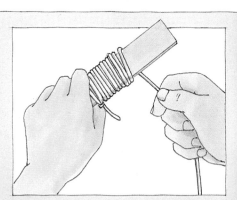

17. Tie one end of the spare nylon cord to the wooden stick, and wind all the cord round it. This is the flying line and handle.

4. Cut 4.5m from the nylon cord.

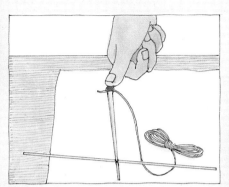

5. Push a drawing pin through one end of this length of cord, and into the bottom of the spine.

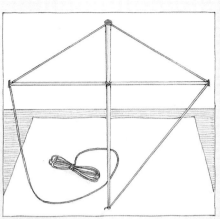

6. Pull the cord tight, and fix it to each of the other three points of the frame with drawing pins.

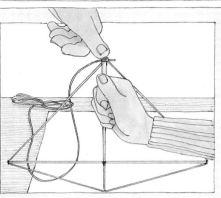

7. At the bottom of the spine, remove the drawing pin and then push it through both thicknesses of cord. The piece left forms the tail.

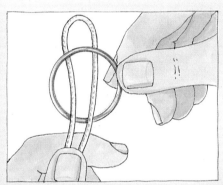

12. Cut 120 cm of cord, fold it in half, and push the looped end through the curtain ring.

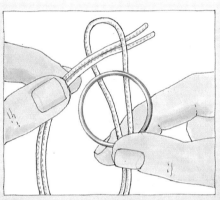

13. Pull the two loose ends back through the loop.

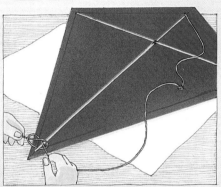

14. Tie one end of the cord to the top of the spine, and the other end to the bottom. This is the bridle.

18. Tie the other end of the cord to the curtain ring.

Try flying the kite when a steady breeze is blowing. Don't fly it near electrical cables or power lines. Spin out a few metres of the flying line. Ask a friend to throw the kite into the air as you run along with the line. If the kite tends to nose-dive, lengthen its tail. If it tends to fall backwards, shorten the tail.

Glossary and index

Words in CAPITAL LETTERS are also defined in the glossary.